Django Cookbook

Web Development with Django

Step by Step Guide

By Logan Barton

Table of Contents

Disclaimer

While all attempts have been made to verify the information provided in this book, the author does assume any responsibility for errors, omissions, or contrary interpretations of the subject matter contained within. The information provided in this book is for educational and entertainment purposes only. The reader is responsible for his or her own actions and the author does not accept any responsibilities for any liabilities or damages, real or perceived, resulting from the use of this information.

**The trademarks that are used are without any consent, and the publication of the trademark is without permission or backing by the trademark owner. All trademarks and brands within this book are for clarifying purposes only and are the owned by the owners themselves, not affiliated with this document. **

Introduction

The need for web apps has been on the rise. However, most languages that support web development do not provide an easy means by which to implement the modern need for web apps. This means that developers spend longer periods of time developing these apps. Django is a Python framework that provides web developers with a mechanism to develop web apps in a quick and easy manner. Therefore you need to know how to use the Python framework. This book explores this in detail. Make sure that you install Python Python 2.6.5 or higher. Enjoy reading!

Chapter 1- The Django Admin Interface

The automatic admin interface in Django is one of its powerful parts. It works by reading metadata from models to provide a model-centric and quick interface in which the trusted users of the site can be in a position to manage their data. This is recommended as the internal management tool of an organization. It is not used for building the whole of the front end for your app.

The admin provides you with several tools for customization, but make sure you use them effectively. If need to create a process-centric interface that highly abstracts the details regarding its implementation such as the database tables, then it will be good for you to begin writing your own views.

In this chapter, we will guide you on how to activate, use and then customize the Django's admin interface.

A Brief Overview

The admin comes enabled in a default project template that is used by "startproject". The requirements include the following:

1. Add the 'django.contrib.admin' to the "INSTALLED_APPS" setting.

2. The admin provides four dependencies, that is, "django.contrib.auth", "django.contrib.contenttypes", "django.contrib.messages" and "django.contrib.sessions". If you do not find these in the "INSTALLED_APPS", then just add them.

3. Add the "django.contrib.messages.context_processors.messages" and "django.contrib.auth.context_processors.auth" to the option "context_processors" of the DjangoTemplates backend that has been defined in the

TEMPLATES and

"django.contrib.auth.middleware.AuthenticanMiddlew

are" and

"django.contrib.messages.middleware.MessageMiddlew

are" to the "MIDDLEWARE_CLASSES".

4. Determine the models in your application that should be editable.

5. For each of the above models, optionally make a "ModelAdmin" class that will encapsulate the customized admin functionality and the options for the particular model.

6. Instantiate "AdminSite" and then inform it about the models and the "ModelAdmin" classes.

7. Hook the instance of "AdminSite" into the URLconf.

Once you have done the above steps, you will be in a position to make use of the Admin interface just by using the URL you hooked into. If you need to create a user to be used for login, then use the command "createsuperuser".

The "modelAdmin" Objects

Class "ModelAdmin"

This class represents a model in the Admin interface. These are stored in a file named "admin.py" in the application. Below is an example of a ModelAdmin:

from django.contrib import admin

from project1.myapplication.models import Author

class AuthorAdmin(admin.ModelAdmin):

   pass

admin.site.register(Author, AuthorAdmin)

The register decorator

This is a decorator, which is used for the purpose of registering the ModelAdmin classes. It is used as shown below:

```
from django.contrib import admin
from .models import Author
@admin.register(Author)
class AuthorAdmin(admin.ModelAdmin):
    pass
```

It is always given one or more model classes for registration with the ModelAdmin and the keyword argument "site", which is optional for those not using AdminSite, the default:

```
from django.contrib import admin
from .models import Author, Reader, Editor
from project1.admin_site import custom_admin_site
```

```
@admin.register(Author, Reader, Editor,
site=custom_admin_site)

class PersonAdmin(admin.ModelAdmin):

    pass
```

The model decorator can be used for referencing the model admin class in the "__init__()" method.

ModelAdmin Options

ModelAdmin is very flexible. It provides you with a number of options that can help you in customization of the interface. The definition of the options is done in the ModelAdmin subclass.

```
from django.contrib import admin
class AuthorAdmin(admin.ModelAdmin):
    date_hierarchy = 'pub_date'
```

ModelAdmin.Actions

This has a list of actions that will be made available on the list page for the change.

ModelAdmin.empty_value_display

This attribute will override the default value for the display for the fields of the record that are empty. Consider the following example:

from django.contrib import admin

class AuthorAdmin(admin.ModelAdmin):

   empty_value_display = '-empty-'

One can also override the "empty_value_display" for all the admin pages, or for some specified fields as shown below:

```python
from django.contrib import admin
class AuthorAdmin(admin.ModelAdmin):
    fields = ('name', 'title', 'view_birth_date')
    def view_birth_date(self, obj):
        return obj.birth_date
    view_birth_date.empty_value_display = '???'
ModelAdmin.exclude:
```

This should have the list of fields that will be excluded from a form. Consider the model given below:

```python
from django.db import models
class Author(models.Model):
    name = models.CharField(max_length=100)
    title = models.CharField(max_length=3)
    birth_date    =    models.DateField(blank=True, null=True)
```

If you need a form for the model that only has the name and the title fields, you may choose to specify the fields you need or exclude these. This is shown below:

```
from django.contrib import admin
class AuthorAdmin(admin.ModelAdmin):
    fields = ('name', 'title')
class AuthorAdmin(admin.ModelAdmin):
    exclude = ('birth_date',)
```

ModelAdmin.fieldsets:

This should be used to control the layout of the admin "change" and "add" pages. Consider the example given below:

```
from django.contrib import admin
class FlatPageAdmin(admin.ModelAdmin):
    fieldsets = (
        (None, {
            'fields': ('url', 'title', 'content', 'sites')
```

```
    }),
    ('Advanced options', {
        'classes': ('collapse',),
        'fields':                    ('registration_required',
'template_name'),
    }),
)
```

The above code should give you an admin page.

In the following example, we have the ModelAdmin and ModelForm defining the exclude option. In such a case, the ModelAdmin should take precedence. This is shown below:

```
from django import forms
from myapp.models import Person
from django.contrib import admin
class PForm(forms.ModelForm):
    class Meta:
        model = Person
```

```
    exclude = ['name']
class PersonAdmin(admin.ModelAdmin):
    exclude = ['age']
    form = PForm
```

The above code will give you a form in which the "name" field is included but the "age" field is excluded.

ModelAdmin.formfield_overrides:

This will provide us with a quick and easy way to override some Field options to be used in the admin. The following example demonstrates how to use this:

```
from django.db import models
from django.contrib import admin
# Import the custom widget and the model from their definition place
from myapplication.widgets import RichTextEditorWidget
from myapplication.models import MyModel
```

```
class MyModelAdmin(admin.ModelAdmin):

    formfield_overrides = {

        models.TextField: {'widget':
RichTextEditorWidget},

    }
```

ModelAdmin.list_display:

The "list_display" should be set for controlling the fields that are to be displayed on the admin page for the change list. This is shown below:

```
list_display = ('first_name', 'last_name')
```

There are four possible values that can be used for "list_display". Let's discuss them:

1. The model field.

   This is shown below:

```
class PAdmin(admin.ModelAdmin):
```

list_display = ('first_name', 'last_name')

2. A callable, which will only accept one parameter for the instance of the model:
   This is shown below:

```
def upper_case_name(obj):
    return ("%s %s" % (obj.first_name,
obj.last_name)).upper()
upper_case_name.short_description = 'Name'
class PAdmin(admin.ModelAdmin):
    list_display = (upper_case_name,)
```

3. A string to represent an attribute on ModelAdmin. This will exhibit a similar behavior to the callable. The following example demonstrates this:

```
class PersonAdmin(admin.ModelAdmin):
    list_display = ('upper_case_name',)
    def upper_case_name(self, obj):
```

```
return ("%s %s" % (obj.first_name,
obj.last_name)).upper()
```

```
upper_case_name.short_description    =
'Name'
```

4. A string to represent an attribute in a model. This exhibits a similar behavior to the callable, but "self" will form the instance of the model. Consider the full example given below:

```
from django.contrib import admin
from django.db import models
class Person(models.Model):
    name = models.CharField(max_length=50)
    birthday = models.DateField()
    def decade_born_in(self):
        return    self.birthday.strftime('%Y')[:3]    +
"0's"
    decade_born_in.short_description   =   'Birth
decade'
class PersonAdmin(admin.ModelAdmin):
    list_display = ('name', 'decade_born_in')
```

ModelAdmin.list_filter:

The "list_filter" should be set for activating the filters in the right sidebar of the change list page for the admin.

The list_filter should be made up of a list of tuple or list elements.

Chapter 2- Writing Views

A view is a web function that usually takes a web request and then gives back a web response. The response in this case can be the web contents in HTML, an XML document, a 404 error, a redirect or an image. The view itself should have any necessary logic that is good for returning the response. The code for the view can be stored anywhere you want, but should be in your Python path. The code for the view should be placed in a file with the name "view.py", and then the file should be kept in the directory for the application or project.

Consider the view given below, which will give us the current date and time in the HTML format:

```
from django.http import HttpResponse
import datetime
def current_datetime(request):
    now = datetime.datetime.now()
```

```
html = "<html><body>It is %s.</body></html>" %
now

return HttpResponse(html)
```

Let's discuss what we have done in the code:

1. We have begun by importing the "HttpResponse" class from the "django.http" module and the "datetime" library for Python.

2. Next, we have defined a function with the name "current_datetime". This is the function for the view. Each view function will take an HttpRequest object as the first parameter, and in this case, we have given it the name "request". However, it's worth noting that any name can be used for the view function. The name doesn't have to be specific so that the Django can recognize it. In our case, we have given the function the name "current_datetime" so that we can indicate exactly what it does.

3. The view will then return an HttpRequest object, and this will have the response that has been generated. Each view function has the responsibility of returning an object of the type "HttpResponse".

Mapping URLs to Views

In our previous example, the view returned a HTML page with both the current date and time. For this view to be displayed on a specific URL, you will have to create a URL conf.

Returning Errors

It is easy to return HTTP error codes in Django. The HttpResponse provides us with a number of subclasses for some Http status codes in addition to the 200, which stands for "ok". The request/response documentation can give you all the available subclasses for this. To signify that you have an error, you just have to return an instance of any of the subclasses. This is shown in the following example:

```
from django.http import HttpResponse,
HttpResponseNotFound

def my_view(request):

    # ...

    if foo:

        return    HttpResponseNotFound('<h1>Page    not
found</h1>')

    else:

        return            HttpResponse('<h1>Page        was
found</h1>')
```

No specialized subclass exists for each of the possible HTTP response codes, since most of these will not be common. Also, the HTTP status codes can be passed into the constructor for our HttpResponse documentation for creation of a return class of any of the status codes. Consider the example given below:

```
from django.http import HttpResponse
def my_view(request):
    # ...
    # Return a "created" (201) response code.
    return HttpResponse(status=201)
```

One can easily handle the 404 errors since these form the common types of errors in HTTP.

The Http404 exception

THE CLASS django.http.Http404:

After returning an error like the "HttpResponseNotFound", you should take the responsibility of definition of the HTML of the error page that result. This is shown below:

return HttpResponseNotFound('<h1>Page not found</h1>')

For convenience purposes, and because it is good to maintain a HTML page for 404 in Django, we are provided with the Http404 exception. Once you have raised the Http404 anywhere in your view, Django will have to catch this and then return a standard error page for the application, and the Http error code for 404. Consider the example that has been given below:

from django.http import Http404

from polls.models import Poll

```
from django.shortcuts import render

def detail(request, poll_id):

    try:

        p = Poll.objects.get(pk=poll_id)

    except Poll.DoesNotExist:

        raise Http404("Poll doesn't exist")

    return render(request, 'polls/detail.html', {'poll': p})
```

If you need to show a customized HTML once the Django returns the 404, you can create a HTML template and then give it the name "404.html", and this should be stored in the top level for your tree. Once the "DEBUG" has been set to "false", the template will be saved.

If the "DEBUG" is "true", you can choose to provide a message for the Http404 and this will be displayed in the standard debug template for 404. Such messages should be used for the purposes of debugging, since they cannot be used in a 404 production template.

Customizing error views

The Django default error views are expected to suffice for most web applications, but overriding these can be done easily if you need any new custom behavior. You should specify the handlers, as shown below in URLconf.

The view "page_not_found()" has been overridden by "handler404". This is shown below:

handler404 = 'mysite.views.custom_page_not_found_view'

The view "server_error()" was overridden by "handler404". This is shown below:

handler500 = 'mysite.views.custom_error_view'

The view "permission_denied()" has been overridden by handler403:

**handler403 =
'mysite.views.custom_permission_denied_view'**

The view "bad_request()" has been overridden by handler400:

**handler400 =
'mysite.views.custom_bad_request_view'**

View Decorators

Django provides us with a number of decorators that we can apply to our views for supporting a number of HTTP features.

Allowed HTTP Methods

We can use the decorators provided in "django.views.decorators.http" for the purpose of restriction of access to the views depending on the request method. If the condition is not fulfilled, then the decorators will have to return: "django.http.HttpResponseNotFound".

require_http_methods:

This is a decorator that requires that a view will only accept some particular view methods. This is used as shown below:

```
from django.views.decorators.http import
require_http_methods

@require_http_methods(["GET", "POST"])

def my_view(request):

    # Now, we can assume that only the GET or the
POST requests make it #this far

    # ...

    pass
```

Chapter 3- File Uploads

Once the Django has handled a file, then this file has to be placed in "request.FILES". This is the file that is responsible for giving an explanation on how the files have been stored in memory and disk, and how the default behavior can be customized.

Consider the basic file upload code given below:

```
from django import forms
class UploadForm(forms.Form):
    title = forms.CharField(max_length=50)
    file = forms.FileField()
```

The view that is responsible for handling the form will get the file data in the "request.FILES", and this is a dictionary that has a key for each of the FileField in our form. This is an indication that the data resulting from the form can be accessed in the form of "request.FILES['file']".

In most cases, you will just have to pass the data for the file from the "request" into your form. This is shown in the following example:

```
from django.http import HttpResponseRedirect
from .forms import UploadFileForm
from django.shortcuts import render
# Imaginary function for handling an uploaded file.
from somewhere import handle_uploaded_file
def upload_file(request):
    if request.method == 'POST':
        form = UploadForm(request.POST,
request.FILES)
        if form.is_valid():
```

```
    handle_uploaded_file(request.FILES['file'])

    return HttpResponseRedirect('/success/url/')

else:

    form = UploadForm()

    return render(request, 'upload.html', {'form':
form})
```

Also, remember that it is necessary to pass "form.FILES" into the constructor of your form, and the data for your file will be bound into the form.

A file can be uploaded as shown below:

```
def handle_uploaded_file(f):

    with    open('some/file/name.txt',    'wb+')    as
destination:

        for chunk in f.chunks():

            destination.write(chunk)
```

Now that we are looping over the method "UploadedFile.chunks()", rather than "read()", we will ensure that the system memory is not overwhelmed even by our large files.

Using a Model to Handle Uploaded Files

If you have a file with "FileField" and you want to save it in a model, the use of "ModelForm" will make it quick and easy for you. The file will have to be saved in the location that you specify in the property "upload_to" in the corresponding "FileField" when you are calling the method "form.save()". This is demonstrated in the code given below:

```
from django.http import HttpResponseRedirect
from .forms import ModelFormFileField
from django.shortcuts import render
def upload_file(request):
    if request.method == 'POST':
        form = ModelFormFileField(request.POST, request.FILES)
        if form.is_valid():
            # file is saved
            form.save()
```

```python
        return HttpResponseRedirect('/success/url/')
    else:
        form = ModelFormFileField()
    return render(request, 'upload.html', {'form': form})
```

If you are manually constructing an object, you can choose to assign the file object from the "request.FILES" into the file field in your model. This is shown in the code given below:

```python
from django.http import HttpResponseRedirect
from .forms import UploadFileForm
from django.shortcuts import render
from .models import ModelWithFileField
def upload_file(request):
    if request.method == 'POST':
        form = UploadForm(request.POST, request.FILES)
        if form.is_valid():
            instance = ModelFileField(file_field=request.FILES['file'])
```

```python
        instance.save()

        return HttpResponseRedirect('/success/url/')
    else:

        form = UploadForm()

    return render(request, 'upload.html', {'form':
form})
```

Uploading multiple files

Sometimes, you may need to use one form so as to upload multiple files. This can be done by setting the "multiple" HTML attribute of the widget field. This is shown below:

```
from django import forms
class FileForm(forms.Form):
    file_field =
forms.FileField(widget=forms.ClearableFileInput(attrs={'multiple': True}))
```

The "post" method of the "FormView" subclass can then be overridden so as to handle the multiple file uploads. This can be done as shown below:

```
from django.views.generic.edit import FormView
from .forms import FileFieldForm
class FileFieldView(FormView):
    form_class = FileForm
```

```python
    template_name = 'upload.html'  # Replace with the
template.
    success_url = '...'  # Replace with the URL or
reverse().
    def post(self, request, *args, **kwargs):
        form_class = self.get_form_class()
        form = self.get_form(form_class)
        files = request.FILES.getlist('file_field')
        if form.is_valid():
            for f in files:
                ...  # Do an action with each file.
            return self.form_valid(form)
        else:
            return self.form_invalid(form)
```

Upload Handlers

Once a user has uploaded a file, Django will pass off the data of the file to "upload handler". This is a small class with the responsibility of handling file data when it is being uploaded. The definition of upload handlers is done in the setting "FILE_UPLOAD_HANDLERS". The setting usually defaults to the following:

["django.core.files.uploadhandler.MemoryFileUploa dHandler",

"django.core.files.uploadhandler.TemporaryFileUplo adHandler"]

Chapter 4- Shortcut Functions

The "django.shortcuts" package in Django helps us collect helper functions and classes that span multiple levels of the MVC. This means that such classes and functions usually introduce controlled coupling for the sake of convenience.

render():

The function combines a specific template and a specific context dictionary and then returns an object of HttpResponse with the rendered text.

The two arguments that are required for this function include the following:

1. request- this is the request object hat is used for the purpose of generating the response.

---

2. template_name- this should be the full name of the template that is to be used, or just a sequence of names for templates. If you provide a sequence of template, the first one to be found will be used.

The following are the other arguments, but they are optional:

1. context- this is a dictionary of values that are to be added to the template context. By default, it is just an empty dictionary. If the dictionary has a value that is callable, then the view will have to call it before it is rendered in the template.

2. context-instance- this is the context instance that is to be rendered with the template. By default, the template will have to be rendered with an instance of RequestInstance.

3. content_type- this is the MIME type that is to be used with the document which results. The default value for it is "DEFAULT_VALUE_TYPE".

4. Status- this is the status code for your response. The default value for this is 200.

5. current_app- this is a hint that tells us the application that has the current view.

6. using- this is the name of the template engine that we should use for the purpose of loading the template.

Consider the example given below:

```
from django.shortcuts import render
def my_view(request):
    # View code should be added here...
    return render(request, 'myapplication/index.html', {
        'foo': 'bar',
    }, content_type='application/xhtml+xml')
```

In the above example, we are rendering the "myapplication/index.html" template with a MIME type application. Below is an equivalent example:

```python
from django.http import HttpResponse

from django.template import loader

def my_view(request):

    # View code should be added here...

    t = loader.get_template('myapplication/index.html')

    c = {'foo': 'bar'}

    return HttpResponse(t.render(c, request), content_type='application/xhtml+xml')
```

redirect()

This will return a "HttpResponseRedirect" to our appropriate URL for arguments that have been passed. The arguments in this can be a model, a name of a view, or a relative or an absolute URL.

The "redirect()" function can be used in a number of ways:

1. By passing an object, the "get-absolute_url()" method for the object will be called for figuring out our redirected URL. This is shown below:

   from django.shortcuts import redirect

   def my_view(request):

   ...

   object = MyModel.objects.get(...)

   return redirect(object)

2. Passing a view name and optional keyword or positional arguments. The provided URL will have to be reverse resolved by use of the "reverse()" method. This is shown below:

```
def my_view(request):
    ...
    return redirect('a-view-name', foo='bar')
```

3. By passing a hardcoded URL we want to redirect to. This is shown below:

```
def my_view(request):
    ...
    return redirect('/some/url/')
```

This can also be applied to full URLs as shown below:

```
def my_view(request):
    ...
```

```
return redirect('https://sample.com/')
```

The default setting is that the "redirect()" method will return a temporary redirect. For the case of forms that accept a "permanent" argument, if we set it to "True", then we will get back a permanent redirect. This is shown below:

```
def my_view(request):
    ...
    object = MyModel.objects.get(...)
    return redirect(object, permanent=True
```

get_object_or_404()

This method will call "get()" on a specified model manager, but it will raise a Http404 error rather than the "DoesNotExist" exception for the model. The following are some of the required arguments for this method:

1. klass- this is a manager, a model class, or a Query instance from which we will get an object.

2. **kwargs- these are the lookup para

3. meters, and these have to be in a format that is accepted by "filter()" or "get()".

Consider the example given below in which we will get an object from MyModl and the object should have a primary key of 2. Here is the example:

from django.shortcuts import get_object_or_404
def my_view(request):

```
my_object = get_object_or_404(MyModel, pk=2)
```

The above example is equivalent to the one given below:

```
from django.http import Http404


def my_view(request):
    try:
        my_object = MyModel.objects.get(pk=2)
    except MyModel.DoesNotExist:
        raise Http404("No MyModel has matched your query.")
```

The common use case for this is passing a model as described above. Also, one can pass an instance of "QuerySet" as shown below:

```
queryset = Book.objects.filter(title__startswith='M')
get_object_or_404(queryset, pk=2)
```

Similarly, the above can be done as follows:

```
get_object_or_404(Book,          title__startswith='M',
pk=2)
```

A Manager can be used as shown below:

```
get_object_or_404(Book.dahl_objects,

title='Matrix')
```

Related managers can be used as shown below:

```
author = Author.objects.get(name='John Joel')

get_object_or_404(author.book_set, title='Matrix')
```

_get_list_or_404()_

This will give us the result of "filter()" on the given model manager that has been casted to a list, raising a Http404 in case the result is found to be empty.

The following are the required arguments for this:

1. klass- this is a manager, a model class, or a Query instance from which we will get an object.

2. **kwargs- these are the lookup parameters, and these have to be in a format that is accepted by "filter()" or "get()".

Consider the example given below in which we will get all the objects that have been published by MyModel:

```python
from django.shortcuts import import get_list_or_404

def my_view(request):

    my_objects    =    get_list_or_404(MyModel,
published=True)
```

The above example is same as the one given below:

```python
from django.http import Http404

def my_view(request):

    my_objects                                =
list(MyModel.objects.filter(published=True))

    if not my_objects:

        raise Http404("No MyModel has matched your
query.")
```

Chapter 5- Models and Databases

A model defines the single and definitive source of information for your data. It has the necessary fields and behaviors for the data which you have stored. In general, each model will map to a single table in a database.

Note that in Django, each model represents a Python class that subclasses the "django.db.models.Model". Each attribute in the model is a representation of a database field. Django provides you with a database API that is generated automatically.

Consider the example given below:

```
from django.db import models
class Person(models.Model):
    first_name = models.CharField(max_length=40)
    last_name = models.CharField(max_length=40)
```

In the above example, we have defined a person having both a "first_name" and a "last_name". These are the fields for the model. This shows that each field has to be defined as an attribute for the class, and each of the attributes has to be mapped to a column in the database.

With the Person model given above, a database will be created as shown below:

CREATE TABLE myapplication_person (

  "id" serial NOT NULL PRIMARY KEY,

  "first_name" varchar(40) NOT NULL,

  "last_name" varchar(40) NOT NULL

);

The field "id" has been added automatically, but it is possible for us to override such a behavior.

Using Models

After the definition of models, you can tell the Django they need to make use of the model. This can be do

ne by editing the file for settings and then changing the setting for "INSTALLED_APPS" so we can add the name of the module having the "modules.py".

Consider a situation in which you have the modules for your application residing in "myapplication.models" module, the "INSTALLED_APPS" should read as follows in part:

INSTALLED_APPS = [

   #...

   'myapplication',

   #...

]

After adding the new apps to INSTALLED_APPS, ensure that you run "manage.py migrate"; this will help you make some migrations.

Fields

The fields of a database form the most important part of the model and the only part of the model that is required. Specification of fields is done using class attributes. It's a good idea to select the names of fields that do not conflict with the ModelAPIs, such as save2, clean and delete.

Consider the example given below:

```
from django.db import models
class Artist(models.Model):
    first_name = models.CharField(max_length=40)
    last_name = models.CharField(max_length=40)
    instrument = models.CharField(max_length=90)
```

```python
class Album(models.Model):

    artist = models.ForeignKey(Artist,
on_delete=models.CASCADE)

    name = models.CharField(max_length=100)

    release_date = models.DateField()

    num_stars = models.IntegerField()
```

Field Types

Each field used in a model should be your appropriate field classes' instance. The field class types in Django are used for determination of a number of things including the following:

1. The type of column, which is responsible for telling the database the type of data that it should store.

2. Default HTM widget, which is used when rendering the form field.

3. Minimal validation requirements, which are used in admin for Django and in the automatically-generated forms.

Django comes with a number of built-in field types. You can write your own fields if the ones provided by Django do not help you to achieve what you need.

Field Options

Each field should take some specific arguments. There are field arguments that can be applied to all of the available field types. The following are the ones that are commonly used:

1. null- if this is true, then the empty database values will be stored as NULL. The default for this is "False".

2. blank- if this is set to "TRUE", then the field will be allowed to be blank. The default value for this is "false".

3. choices- this is an iterable made up of 2 tuples that is to be used as choices for the field.

A choices list should be as shown below:

YEAR_IN_COLLEGE_CHOICES = (

('FR', 'Fresher'),

('NW', 'New'),

('JR', 'Junior'),

('SR', 'Senior'),

('GR', 'Graduate'),

)

The first element in each of the tuples represents the value that will be stored in the database. The second element in this will have to be shown by our default form widget. Consider the example given below:

```
from django.db import models
class Person(models.Model):
    SHIRT_SIZES = (
        ('S', 'Small'),
        ('M', 'Medium'),
        ('L', 'Large'),
    )
    name = models.CharField(max_length=60)
    shirt_size = models.CharField(max_length=1,
choices=TROUSER_SIZES)
```

```
>>> p = Person(name="John Joel", shirt_size="L")
>>> p.save()
>>> p.shirt_size
'L'
>>> p.get_shirt_size_display()
'Large'
```

4. default- this represents the default value for a field. This can be a callable object or just a value. If it is a callable object, then it will have to be called after creation of a new object.

5. help_text- this is the extra "help" text that is to be displayed with your form widget. It is of great importance in documentation, even for those not using it on their form.

6. primary_key- if this is set to "True" for a field, then the field will become the primary key for the model. It's worth remembering that the value for a primary key is

read-only. If the value of a primary key in a field is changed on an object and then saved, then a new object will have to be created alongside the old one. This is demonstrated below:

```
from django.db import models
class Fruit(models.Model):
    name = models.CharField(max_length=90, primary_key=True)
```

```
>>> fruit = Fruit.objects.create(name='Mango')
>>> fruit.name = 'Pear'
>>> fruit.save()
>>> Fruit.objects.values_list('name', flat=True)
['mango', 'Pear']
```

Verbose Field Names

Most field types will always take the first positional argument, which is a verbose name. If the verbose name is not given, Django will have to create it automatically using the attribute name for the field, and the underscores will be converted into spaces.

Consider the example given below:

first_name = models.CharField("first name of person", max_length=30)

In the above example, we have the verbose name as "first name of person". Consider the next example given below:

first_name = models.CharField(max_length=30)

In the above example, the verbose name is "first name".

Consider the next example given below:

```
poll = models.ForeignKey(
    Poll,
    on_delete=models.CASCADE,
    verbose_name="a related poll",
)
sites = models.ManyToManyField(Site,
verbose_name="list of sites")
place = models.OneToOneField(
    Place,
    on_delete=models.CASCADE,
    verbose_name="some related place",
)
```

In the above example, we are using the first argument as the model class, and that is why we have used the argument "verbose_name" keyword.

Relationships

Relational databases greatly help us when relating tables to each other. In Django, we are provided with mechanisms that can help us define the three common types of database relationships.

Many-to-one relationships

The definition of this type of relationship is done using "django.db.models.ForeignKey". This is used directly like any other type of field. A positional argument is required for the ForeignKey, and this should be set to the class to which the model is related.

Consider the example given below:

```
from django.db import models
class Manufacturer(models.Model):
    # ...
```

```
    pass

class Vehicle(models.Model):

    manufacturer = models.ForeignKey(Manufacturer,
on_delete=models.CASCADE)

    # ...
```

It is also possible for anyone to create recursive relationships. In most cases, it is recommended that the name of the field for the primary key should be the name for the model and should be written in lowercase. Note that the model can be given any name.

Consider the example given below:

```
Class Vehicle(models.Model):

    company_which_makes_it = models.ForeignKey(

    Manufacturer,

    on_delete=models.CASCADE,

)

    # ...
```

Many-to-many relationships

The "ManyToManyField" is used for definition of the many-to-many relationship. This should be used just like with any type of field, just as an inclusion of this as the class model. Consider the example given below:

```
from django.db import models
class Topping(models.Model):
    # ...
    pass
class Chips(models.Model):
    # ...
    toppings = models.ManyToManyField(Topping)
```

In the above example, we have the Chips, and this has multiple topping objects.

Extra fields in many-to-many relationships

In our previous examples, we have dealt with the simple many-to-many relationships. However, in some cases, you may need to associate data between two models. In such a case, the Django will give you a chance to specify the model that will take the responsibility of governing the many-to-many relationship. The extra fields can be added in the intermediate model. The intermediate model has to be associated with "ManyToManyField" by use of the "through" argument so as to point to our model, which should act as the intermediary. For the Artist example, we will have the following code:

from django.db import models

class Person(models.Model):

  name = models.CharField(max_length=128)

```python
    def __str__(self):          # __unicode__ on Python
2
        return self.name

class Group(models.Model):

    name = models.CharField(max_length=128)

    members = models.ManyToManyField(Person,
through='Membership')

    def __str__(self):          # __unicode__ on Python
2
        return self.name


class Membership(models.Model):

    person = models.ForeignKey(Person,
on_delete=models.CASCADE)

    group = models.ForeignKey(Group,
on_delete=models.CASCADE)

    date_joined = models.DateField()

    invite_person = models.CharField(max_length=64)
```

After setting up an intermediary model, you should explicitly specify the foreign keys to models that are involved in many-to-many relationships. Such an explicit declaration will specify the relationship between the two models we have.

The following are the restrictions on the intermediate model:

1. The intermediate model must have one, and only one, foreign key to your source model, or you have to explicitly specify foreign keys to be used by Django for the relationship by use of "ManyToManyField.through_fields". In case you are having more than one foreign key and you have not specified the "through_fields", you will get a validation error. The same restriction will be applied to the foreign key of the target model.

2. For a model having a Many-to-Many relationship to itself via an intermediary model, two foreign keys are

permitted to a similar model, but these have to be taken as the two sides for the many-to-many relationship.

3. Whenever you are defining a many-to-many relationship from a particular model itself, by use of an intermediary model, you must use the "symmetrical=False".

Now that you have set the ManyToManyField to be used for the intermediary model, you will begin to create many-to-many relationships. This can be done by creating instances to the model:

```
>>> john = Person.objects.create(name="John Joel")

>>> paul = Person.objects.create(name="Paul McCarthy")

>>> boscos = Group.objects.create(name="The Boscos")

>>> m1 = Membership(person=john, group=boscos,

...    date_joined=date(2015, 6, 20),

...    invite_reason="Need a new drummer.")

>>> m1.save()
```

```
>>> bosco.members.all()

[<Person: John Joel>]

>>> john.group_set.all()

[<Group: The Boscos>]

>>> m2 = Membership.objects.create(person=paul,
group=boscos,

...    date_joined=date(2014, 7, 5),

...    invite_reason="Want to create a band.")

>>> boscos.members.all()

[<Person: John Joel>, <Person: Paul McCarthy>]
```

However, it will be impossible for you to use the "add", "create", or the assignment, for the purpose of creation of the relationships. This is shown below:

```
# THIS WON'T WORK
>>> boscos.members.add(Benard)
# THIS WON'T WORK EITHER
>>> boscos.members.create(name="George Bush")
# AND NEITHER WILL THIS
```

```
>>> boscos.members = [benard, paul, john, george]
```

You need to ask yourself why you cannot create a relationship between yourself and the group, but you have to create all the details regarding the relationship that is required by the Membership model. The "add", "create" and the "assignment" will not provide us with details regarding this. Due to this, these are usually disabled for the many-to-many relationships that make use of the intermediate model. For this type of relationship to be created, we have to make instances for the intermediate model.

The "remove ()" method has also been disabled. We can use the "clear()" method for removal of many-to-many relationships for our instance. This is shown in the code given below:

```
>>> # BOscoss have been broken up
>>> boscos.members.clear()
```

>>> # Note that this will delete the instances of the intermediate model

>>> Membership.objects.all()

[]

After the establishment of the many-to-many relationships by creation of instances for the intermediate models, you will be in a position to issue queries. Just like in the regular many-to-many relationships, one can query using the attributes of the model related to the many-to-many relationship. This is shown below:

 # Find all groups having a member whith a name starting with 'Paul'

>>> Group.objects.filter(members__name__startswith=' Paul')

[<Group: The Boscos>]

Since you are using the intermediate model, you are allowed to query the attributes. This is shown below:

Find all members of the Boscos who joined after 1 Jan 2010

```
>>> Person.objects.filter(
...    group__name='The Boscos',
...    membership__date_joined__gt=date(2010,1,1))
[<Person: John Joel]
```

If you need to access the membership information, you just have to query the Membership model as shown below:

```
>>> john_membership = Membership.objects.get(group=boscos, person=john)
>>> john_membership.date_joined
datetime.date(2015, 7, 20)
>>> john_membership.invite_reason
'Need a new drummer.'
```

Querying your many-to-many relationships from the object "Person" can also access the same information. This is shown below:

```
>>> john_membership =
john.membership_set.get(group=boscos)

>>> john_membership.date_joined

datetime.date(2015, 7, 20)

>>> john_membership.invite_reason

'Need a new drummer.'
```

Models across files

It is possible and a good idea to relate a particular model to another one from another app. For this to be done, you should import the related model at the top of your file where the definition of the model has been done. You can then refer to the rest of the model class where it is needed. Consider the example given below:

```
from django.db import models

from geography.models import ZipCode

class Hotel(models.Model):
```

```
# ...

zip_code = models.ForeignKey(

    ZipCode,

    on_delete=models.SET_NULL,

    blank=True,

    null=True,

)
```

Field Name Restrictions

In Django, only two restrictions are placed in the model field names. These include the following:

1. A field name in Python cannot be a reversed word, because this will give a Python syntax error. Consider the example given below:

   class Sample(models.Model):

   pass = models.IntegerField() # 'pass' is just a reserved word!

2. A field name cannot have more than one underscore in a row, because of the way the query lookup syntax in Django works. This is shown in the following example:

class Sample(models.Model):

  foo__bar = models.IntegerField() # 'foo__bar' is having two underscores!

We can work around the limitations, but the name of the field must not match the name of the database column.

Meta options

A model can be given metadata using the inner class meta, as shown below:

```
from django.db import models
class Bull(models.Model):
    horn_length = models.IntegerField()
    class Meta:
        ordering = ["horn_length"]
        verbose_name_plural = "bull"
```

The Model metadata should be anything that is not a field, such as the ordering options, the database table name, or the human-readable plural and singular names.

Model methods

Custom methods should be defined on a model for addition of low level functionality to our objects. Although the intention of Manager methods is to do things that are table-wide, the model methods are intended to work on a specific model instance. This is an excellent technique for when you need to keep the logic of business in one place, which is the model. Consider the model given below for some custom methods:

```
from django.db import models
class Person(models.Model):
    first_name = models.CharField(max_length=60)
    last_name = models.CharField(max_length=60)
    birth_date = models.DateField()

    def baby_status(self):
        "Returns the baby status for a person."
        import datetime
```

```python
        if self.birth_date < datetime.date(1951, 7, 1):

            return "Pre-boomer"

        elif self.birth_date < datetime.date(1965, 2, 1):

            return "Baby boomer"

        else:

            return "Post-boomer"


    def _get_full_name(self):

        "Returns the full name of a person."

        return '%s %s' % (self.first_name, self.last_name)

    full_name = property(_get_full_name)
```

Overriding Model Methods

Another set of model methods exist that encapsulate some of the database behavior that you will need to customize. In most cases, you will need to change how the "save()" and "delete()" methods work. To change the behavior for the methods, you have to override the methods themselves. Feel free to override such methods so that you can alter the behavior of such methods.

Suppose that you need to have something happen whenever you have saved an object. This is a good opportunity to override the behavior of the "save()" method. Consider the code given below, which shows how this can be implemented:

```python
from django.db import models
class Web(models.Model):
    name = models.CharField(max_length=90)
    tagline = models.TextField()
```

```
def save(self, *args, **kwargs):

   do_something()

   super(Web, self).save(*args, **kwargs)
# Call the exact "save()" method.

   perform_an_action_else()
```

If you need to prevent saving from occurring, then you can do as follows:

```
from django.db import models
class Web(models.Model):
   name = models.CharField(max_length=90)
   tagline = models.TextField()
   def save(self, *args, **kwargs):
      if self.name == "My own blog":
         return # He will never have his own blog!
      else:
         super(Blog, self).save(*args, **kwargs)
# Call the "exact" save() method.
```

Abstract base classes

These types of classes are of great importance when you need to add some common information into several models. The base class is written and then you add "abstract=True" in your Meta class. Such a model will not be used for the purpose of creation of any database table. Instead, after using it as the base model for the other models, the fields it has will have to be added to those of the child class. Note that presence of fields in the abstract base classes similar to the child classes is an error.

Consider the example given below:

from django.db import models

class CommonInformation(models.Model):

   name = models.CharField(max_length=100)

   age = models.PositiveIntegerField()

   class Meta:

```
    abstract = True

class Student(CommonInformation):

  home_group = models.CharField(max_length=5)
```

The above student model will have 3 fields, that is, the name, age and home_group. The model "CommonInformation" cannot be used by the Django model as a normal model since it has been used as an abstract base class. It will also not generate a database table, or maybe have a manager, and we cannot save or instantiate it directly.

Most people are in need of such a model in most of the use cases. If a child fails to declare its own Meta class, then it will have to inherit the meta for the parent. This provides us with an easy mechanism for factoring out some specific information at the Python level, and we will continue with creating a single database table for each child at the database level.

Meta Inheritance

After creation of an abstract base class, Django will make any Meta inner class that you had declared in the base class to be available just as an attribute. If a child fails to perform a declaration of its own Meta class, then it will have to inherit the one from its parent. If the child needs to inherit the Meta class of the parent, it can choose to subclass it. The example given below demonstrates how this can be done:

```
from django.db import models
class CommonInformation(models.Model):
    # ...
    class Meta:
        abstract = True
        ordering = ['name']
class Student(CommonInformation):
    # ...
    class Meta(CommonInformation.Meta):
```

```
db_table = 'student_info'
```

Django has to make one adjustment to Meta class of abstract base class, that is, before the Meta attribute is installed, the property "abstract=False" has to be set. This is an indication that the children of the abstract base class do not automatically become abstract. It is possible for one to create an abstract base class that will inherit from another abstract base class. You just need to set the property "abstract=True" each time that you need to do this.

Sometimes, you may be using the attribute "related_name" on "manyToManeField" or "ForeignKey". In such cases, you are expected to specify a reverse name for your field. This would cause problems in the abstract base classes, since our fields on such classes have been included into the child classes, with similar values for the attributes each of the time.

Suppose you have the following code for the application "common/models.py":

from django.db import models

```python
class Base(models.Model):

    m2m = models.ManyToManyField(OtherModel,
related_name="%(app_label)s_%(class)s_related")
    class Meta:

        abstract = True

class ChildX(Base):

    pass

class ChildZ(Base):

    pass
```

And another app "rare/models.py", which is shown below:

```python
from common.models import Base

class ChildZ(Base):

    pass
```

In such a case, the reverse name for the field "common.ChildX.m2m" will be the "common_childx_related", while the reverse name for the field "common.ChildZ.m2m" will be the "common_childz_related" and finally, the field "rare.ChildZ.m2m" will have the reverse name as the "rare_childz_related".

Multi-table inheritance

Django supports a type of inheritance in which you have each model contained in the hierarchy being a model itself. Note that each of models has a corresponding database table and this can be created or queried individually. The inheritance relationship introduces a link between the child model and each of the parents. Consider the example given below:

```
from django.db import models
class Location(models.Model):
    name = models.CharField(max_length=60)
    address = models.CharField(max_length=70)
```

```
class Hotel(Place):

    serves_hot_dogs                                =
models.BooleanField(default=False)

    serves_chips                                   =
models.BooleanField(default=False)
```

In the above example, all the fields for "Loication" will be present in the "Hotel", but the data will be residing in a different database table. This means that the following are possible:

>>> Location.objects.filter(name="John's Cafe")

>>> Hotel.objects.filter(name="John's Cafe")

If you have a "Location" that is still a "Hotel", you can make use of the lower version of the name of the model to get from the "Location" object to the "Hotel" object. This is shown below:

>>> p = Location.objects.get(id=12)

 # If p is a Hotel object, this will give your child class:

>>> p.hotel

<Hotel: ...>

However, if the "p" in the above case is not a Hotel, then referring to "p.Hotel" will cause an exception named "Hotel.DoesNotExist".

Meta and multi-table inheritance

In a situation where we have the multi-table inheritance, it will not make any sense for a child class to inherit from a subclass of the Meta class of the parent. Since all of the available Meta options have been applied to the parent class, once we apply them for the second time, we will only be creating some contradictory behavior.

A child model is not allowed to have access to the Meta class of the parent. However, some cases exist in which a child just inherits some behavior from the parent, and when the child fails to specify the ordering attribute or the "get_latest_by" attribute, it will have to inherit them from the parent.

If there is an ordering in the parent and you don't need the child to have any form of ordering, this can be disabled explicitly as shown below:

```
class ChildModel(ParentModel):
    # ...
    class Meta:
        # Remove ordering effect of the parent
        ordering = []
```

Inheritance and reverse relations

Since the multi-table inheritance makes use of an implicit "OneToOneField" for linking the child to the parent, it means that we are capable of moving down from the parent to the child, as we have demonstrated in our previous example. However, in such a case, we will make use of the name that is the default name for "relate_name" for ForeignKey and ManyToManyField Relationship. If you have chosen to add the above relations to the subclass of your parent model, then the "relate_name" attribute has to be specified for each of the fields. If you forget to do this, then the Django will give you a validation error.

Consider the example given below in which we will use the "Location" class we had to create a new ManyToManyField relationship. Here is the code for this:

class Supplier(Location):

customers = models.ManyToManyField(Location)

The above will give you an error as shown below:

**Reverse query name for 'Supplier.customers' clashes with reverse query
name for 'Supplier.location_ptr'.**

**HINT: Add or change a related_name argument to the definition for
'Supplier.customers' or 'Supplier.location_ptr'.**

Once you add the "relate_name" to the field for customers,

you will have resolved the error.

Proxy Models

Whenever you are using the multi-table inheritance, then a new database table will have to be created for each of the subclass of the model. This behavior is usually the desired one, and the subclass is in need of a place for storing any additional data fields which are not present in the base class. However, sometimes people only need to make a change to the Python behavior of the model, for example to add a new method or change your default manager.

This is what is represented by the proxy model inheritance, that is, creation of a proxy for your original model. The instances of the proxy model can be updated, deleted or created. Remember that all of your data will be saved just as it would when using an original model. The difference is that you can change things just like the default ordering of the model or default manager in proxy, with no need to alter the original.

Declaration of the proxy models is done similarly to the normal models. To tell Django that you have declared a proxy model, you have to set the "proxy" attribute of your Meta class to a "True".

An example of this is when you need to add a new method to Person model. This can be done as shown below:

```python
from django.db import models
class Person(models.Model):
    first_name = models.CharField(max_length=40)
    last_name = models.CharField(max_length=40)
class NewPerson(Person):
    class Meta:
        proxy = True

    def perform_something(self):
        # ...
        Pass
```

The class "NewPerson" will have to operate on the same database table as its parent "Person" class. Also, any of the newly created instances of Person will be accessible via the "NewPerson" class, and vice versa. This is shown below:

>>> p = Person.objects.create(first_name="foo")

>>> NewPerson.objects.get(first_name="foo")

<NewPerson: foobar>

You can also use a proxy model for definition of a different default ordering on the model. You won't always need ordering of the Person model, but if you have used the proxy, ensure that you use the "last_name" attribute so as to order it. This is shown below:

class OrderPerson(Person):
   class Meta:
      ordering = ["last_name"]
      proxy = True

Proxy model managers

If you fail to specify the model managers on the proxy model, it will have to inherit the managers from the parent models. If a manager is defined for the proxy model, then it will be made the default, although the managers that had been defined in the default class will still be available.

Considering our previous example, you can change the default manager at the time of querying the Person model as shown below:

```
from django.db import models
class NewManager(models.Manager):
    # ...
    pass


class NewPerson(Person):
    objects = NewManager()
```

class Meta:

   proxy = True

If you need to add a new manager to your proxy, with no replacement for the existing default, there are necessary techniques that can be used for such a purpose. You just have to create a base class that has the managers and then inherit that after your primary base class. This is shown in the code given below:

```
# Create the abstract class for your new manager.
class ExtraManagers(models.Model):
    secondary = NewManager()
    class Meta:
        abstract = True
class NewPerson(Person, ExtraManagers):
    class Meta:
        proxy = True
```

You don't need to always do this, but it is possible when you need to.

Multiple Inheritance

With the Django models, you can easily inherit from the multiple parent models just like in sub-classing in Python. However, remember that you have to adhere to the Python's resolution rules. The first base class in which a specified name appears will become the one to be used, meaning that if multiple parents have a Meta class, you will only use the first one of these, and the rest will have to be ignored.

In general, you don't need to inherit from some multiple parents. This is highly applicable in "mix-in" classes, that is, addition of a new method or field to each class inheriting the mix-in. It is always good to ensure that your inheritance hierarchies are kept as simple as possible so that you don't create a hard time for yourself when determining the source of particular information.

Note that trying to inherit from multiple models having the same "id" primary key field will lead to an error. If you need to use multiple inheritances properly, make use of an explicit AutoField in your base models. This is demonstrated below:

```
class MyArticle(models.Model):

    article_id = models.AutoField(primary_key=True)

    ...

class Journal(models.Model):

    journal_id = models.AutoField(primary_key=True)

    ...


class JournalReview(Journak, Article):

    pass
```

You can also make use of a common ancestor for the purpose of holding the AutoField. This is shown below:

```
class Piece(models.Model):
    pass
class Article(Piece):
    ...
class Journal(Piece):
    ...
class JournalReview(Journal, Article):
    pass
```

Chapter 6- Django Template Language

This is good for individuals experienced in using of HTML. A template can be seen as just a text file. When using this, you can generate any text-based format such as CSV, XML and HTML. A template has variables, and these are replaced with values once the template has been evaluated, and the tags, which are responsible for evaluation of the template language.

Consider the simple template given below:

```
{% extends "base.html" %}
{% block title %}{{ section.title }}{% endblock %}
{% block content %}
<h1>{{ section.title }}</h1>
{% for story in story_list %}
<h2>
  <a href="{{ story.get_absolute_url }}">
   {{ story.headline|upper }}
```

```
  </a>
</h2>
<p>{{ story.tease|truncatewords:"100" }}</p>
{% endfor %}
{% endblock %}
```

Variables

Variables are defined as "{{ variable }}". Whenever our template engine has met a variable, it will evaluate the variable that will then be replaced with the result. The name of a variable should be a combination of alphanumeric characters and an underscore (_). The variables sections also allow the use of dot (.), but this has a special meaning as discussed below:

Once the template system has encountered a dot, it will perform lookups in the following order:

1. Dictionary lookup.

2. Method or Attribute lookup.

3. Numeric index lookup.

If the value that results is callable, it will be called with no arguments. The result of our call will then become our template value.

The above order of the lookup may result into unexpected behavior with the objects that override the dictionary lookup. To give an example of this, consider the code given below, which shows some code that is an attempt to loop over "collections.defaultdict". Here is the code:

```
{% for j, v in defaultdict.iteritems %}
    Do something with the j and v here...
{% endfor %}
```

Because the dictionary lookup has happened first, the behavior will kick in and then provide a value instead of having to use the intended method ".iteritems()". In such a case, it is recommended that you convert it into a dictionary first.

In the example given above, the "{{ section.title }}" will have to be replaced with the attribute "title" of the object "section".

If you make use of a variable that is not in existence, then the template system will have to insert the "string_if_invalid" option, which will then be set to an empty string, that is, '', by default.

Note that a "bar" in a template expression such as "{{ foo.bar }}" will be seen as a literal string and will not use the value of variable "bar" if one is available in our template context.

Filters

Variables can be filtered by use of filters. The filters appear as "{{ name|lower }}". It will display the value of the variable "{{ name }}" after it has been filtered through the filter "lower", and with this, the text will be converted into lowercase. If you need to apply a filter, just use the pipe (|) character.

It is possible for us to chain filters, meaning that the output from one filter will have to be applied to the next filter. Note that there are some filters that will take in some arguments. There are about 60 built-in filters in Django. Let's discuss the most commonly used template filters in Django:

Default

If your variable has been set to false or empty, then make use of the given default. Otherwise, feel free to make use of the value of the variable. Consider the example given below:

{{ value|default:"nothing" }}

If the "value" has not been provided or is empty, then the above code will give "nothing" as the result.

Length

This will return the length of a particular value. It works for both lists and strings. Consider the example given below:

{{ value|length }}

If you have the value as "['w', 'x', 'y', 'z']", then you will get 4 as the result.

Tags

Tags are written as "{% tag %}". Tags are a bit complex when compared to variables. Some of them will create text in output, others will do control the flow by performing logic or loops, and others will load external information into a template that is to be used later by the variables.

In some tags, the beginning and the ending is needed. Django comes with about 2 dozens of template tags that are built-in. Let's discuss some commonly used tags.

For

This allows us to loop over each of the items that are contained in an array. Consider the example given below in which we need to display athletes from the "athletes":

```
<ul>
```

```
{% for athlete in athletes %}

    <li>{{ athlete.name }}</li>

{% endfor %}

</ul>
```

"if", "elif" and "else"

In this case, a variable is evaluated, and in case it is found to be true, then the block contents will be displayed. Consider the example given below:

```
{% if athletes %}

    Number of athletes: {{ athletes|length }}

{% elif athlete_in_locker_room_list %}

    Athletes should be getting out of locker room very soon!

{% else %}

    No athletes.

{% endif %}
```

In case the "athletes" is not empty, then we will get the number of athletes as the result. This will be done by the variable named "{{ athletes|length }}".

One can employ the mechanism of filters and the various operators in the "if" tag. This is shown below:

```
{% if athletes|length > 1 %}

    Team: {% for athlete in athletes %} ... {% endfor %}
{% else %}

    Athlete: {{ athletes.0.name }}
{% endif %}
```

Template Inheritance

The part of the template engine that is more complex in Django is the template inheritance. This technique allows you to create a skeleton of a template that will have all the elements of our site and will also define the blocks that your child templates will have to override.

Consider the following example, which demonstrates how template inheritance happens:

```html
<!DOCTYPE html>
<html lang="en">
<head>
  <link rel="stylesheet" href="style.css" />
  <title>{% block title %}My Website{% endblock %}</title>
</head>

<body>
```

```
<div id="sidebar">
  {% block sidebar %}
  <ul>
    <li><a href="/">Home</a></li>
    <li><a href="/blog/">Blog</a></li>
  </ul>
  {% endblock %}
</div>

<div id="content">
  {% block content %}{% endblock %}
</div>
</body>
</html>
```

You can give the above template the name "basetemplate.html". We have used it to create a simple HTML skeleton that we are able to use for two-column page.

The use of the "block" tag in the above example enables us create three blocks that can be filled by the child templates.

A child template might be as shown below:

```
{% extends "basetemplate.html" %}
{% block title %}My blog{% endblock %}
{% block content %}
{% for entry in blog_entries %}
   <h2>{{ entry.title }}</h2>
   <p>{{ entry.body }}</p>
{% endfor %}
{% endblock %}
```

The tag "extends" forms the key in this case. It informs the template engine that we are extending another template. After the template system has evaluated this template, it will first have to locate the parent, which is the "basetemplate.html".

The three block tags in the basetemplate.html will be noticed, and these will have to be replaced with the contents of child template. The output will be as shown below, but this will be determined by the value of the "blog_entries". This is shown below:

```
<!DOCTYPE html>
<html lang="en">
<head>
  <link rel="stylesheet" href="style.css" />
  <title>My blog</title>
</head>
<body>
  <div id="sidebar">
    <ul>
      <li><a href="/">Home</a></li>
      <li><a href="/blog/">Blog</a></li>
    </ul>
  </div>
  <div id="content">
```

```
      <h2>Entry one</h2>

      <p>My first entry.</p>

      <h2>Entry two</h2>

      <p>My second entry.</p>

   </div>

</body>

</html>
```

Note that our child template had not defined the sidebar block, and this is why we have used the value from the parent template. Any content within the tag "{% block %}" in the parent template will be used as a fallback always.

Automatic HTML escaping

Whenever we are generating some HTML from our templates, there is a risk that the variable will include characters that will affect the HTML that results. Consider the template fragment given below:

Hello, {{ name }}

The above way seems to be harmless when we are displaying the name of a user, but consider the example shown below of how a user could have entered their name:

<script>alert('hello')</script>

With such a value for the name, the template will be displayed as shown below:

Hello, <script>alert('hello')</script>

With the above, you will get a pop up box from the browser. Consider the example given below in which our name has the "<" symbol:

\<b\>username

In such a case, you will have a template displayed as follows:

Hello, \<b\>username

However, you may not be interested in auto-escaping, in which case you can turn it off.

If you need to turn off auto-escaping for an individual variable, make use of the "safe" filter as shown below:

This has been escaped: {{ data }}

This has not been escaped: {{ data|safe }}

The "safe" should be thought of as a short form for "safe from escaping" and we can interpret it as HTML. If our data has '<b>', you will get the following as the output:

This has been escaped: <b>

This has not been escaped: <b>

For Template Blocks

If you have a template and you need to control auto-escaping, just wrap the template in autoescape tag. This is shown below:

{% autoescape off %}

  Hello {{ name }}

{% endautoescape %}

The tag should take either "on" or "off" as the argument. To force auto-escape, do as shown below:

Auto-escaping is turned on by default. Hello {{ name }}

{% autoescape off %}

  We will not auto-escape this: {{ data }}.

  Nor this: {{ other_data }}

{% autoescape on %}

Auto-escaping will apply again: {{ name }}

{% endautoescape %}

{% endautoescape %}

The use of auto-escaping tag passes the effect to the templates that are extending the current one and the ones that have been included via the "include" tag. Consider the following example:

basetemplate.html:

{% autoescape off %}

<h1>{% block title %}{% endblock %}</h1>

{% block content %}

{% endblock %}

{% endautoescape %}

child.html:

{% extends "base.html" %}

{% block title %}and{% endblock %}

{% block content %}{{ greeting }}{% endblock %}

Since we have turned off auto-escaping in the base template, it will also be disabled in the child and we will get the following HTML:

<h1>and; that</h1>

Hello!

Conclusion

We have come to the end of this book. The Django's admin interface is of great importance for the purpose of performing administrative tasks. The Django's admin comes enabled by default. It works by reading the data from the models so as to give you a quick interface. Although most people think that this is used for developing the whole of the front end of an app, this is not the case. Views are also useful for providing the user with a good interface and in presentation of data to the users. Take advantage of these to present a process-centric data to your users. Forms are a common way of collecting data from the user in any web app. For such forms, developers need to come up with a way for uploading files to the server. Django supports this, allowing you to upload multiple files at once by use of a single form. Implementation of this is easy, as has been discussed in this book. Django also supports the use of models and databases for storage of data.